Answering
Your Wake-Up Call

How to Snap Back From an
Unwanted Life Change and Thrive Again

Answering
Your Wake-Up Call

How to Snap Back From an
Unwanted Life Change and Thrive Again

Ed Oakley, MS, CSP

ENLIGHTENED
LEADERSHIP
PUBLICATIONS

Why Should You Read Answering Your Wake-Up Call

"Left to your own devices, it would take several lifetimes to achieve the transformation Life's New Game has inspired in me in such a short time. I guarantee your life will never look the same. Together, we unlocked doors to insights, clarity, centeredness, personal power, confidence, freedom, and peace."

~ Kelly Oliver, CEO
Business Loan Solutions

"My life has changed dramatically with the help of your work. My business has exploded, and it is on the verge of taking a whole new direction. It is important for us to realize we are not victims but creators of our reality. I want to thank you so much for your support and assistance in my personal growth and development."

~ Ron Schlegel, Transformational Coach and Intuitive
RiseAboveTrauma.com

"Life's New Game has been amazing. Though we were already successful, our consulting business literally quadrupled almost overnight when we started experiencing Ed Oakley's work and so did the value our clients received!"

~ Drs. Karen and Darwin Perkins
Dr-Perkins.com

"Ed's work (Life's New Game) over the past three years added even more fuel to my ability to connect, perform, and transform my clients and audience. Ed's understanding and mastery of the nonphysical "technology" that connects you with your true Power is beyond comprehension until he guides you to experience, understand, practice, and integrate it into your life. When you've struggled long enough, connect with Ed, and discuss how you can leave those struggles behind so that you are free to accomplish your mission in life."

~ Mark S. A. Smith, Business Growth Strategist
BijaCo.com

"I have been working with Ed Oakley as a coach aligning business and spiritual practices for two-and-a-half months. I love my life and the work changes me, my business, my life, all for the better!"

~ Michelle Royal, Chief Innovation Officer
Ridg.com

"I have worked closely with Ed Oakley and Life's New Game for the past five years, experiencing phenomenal growth and clearing of major impediments to growth in many areas of my life, both business and personal."

~ Don McCrea, PhD
YourBusinessLegacy.net

Ed Oakley is a very powerful ally, one that can show you how to quickly and effortlessly realign yourself with your biggest dreams and aspirations."

~ Joshua Phair, Chief Visionary Officer
LucisDollar.io

"*This work has empowered me to take my destiny into my own hands. For me, it has helped remove blocks and gain clarity on big decisions so I could move forward powerfully with ease, joy, and certainty. I would recommend Life's New Game to anyone looking to accelerate their life's purpose and unleash the power of who they really are.*"

~ Karen Rowe, Ghostwriter and Chief Creative Officer
KarenRowe.com

"*I want you to know that I have made it a habit for about three weeks now, to read every morning and every evening before I sleep, the Enlightened Transformation process. I've had amazing shifts in my energy, and it's been easier to release the default thoughts that don't serve me anymore around fear of getting bigger in the world. So thank you, thank you, thank you for your beautiful gifts and compassionate heart.*"

~ Donna Colfer, AFC, CMC
BuildingWealthFromWithin.com

"*Ed Oakley is the real deal. His clearing process (Enlightened Transformation) is outstanding and has actually taken years off my life. And when it comes to measuring Consciousness and Connection to Source, I have been amazed at the information he has been able to provide me, as well as the connection I feel when he is doing his magic.*"

~ Kathy Perry, Social Media &
Facebook Advertising Consultant
KathyPerry.com

""The experience I have had through Life's New Game clearing is immeasurable. I had so many worries and was not believing in myself. I can say that I have overcome worries and feel more positive about what I can do as I continue the process. The love of God is truly felt in everything and around me. I am grateful and thankful for everything."

~ Isabella Effon, General Manager
Taste of South Africa

"I believe in your authenticity and integrity and in Enlightened Transformation (ET). I believe you have been given a real gift from the universe that needs to be shared with others! I trust the energy that I personally feel in my body both during the Mastery Circle experience and yesterday when we spoke on the phone. I also feel a deep shift in me and am very grateful to you and ET."

~ Marigrace Gleason

"I'll admit, I was skeptical at first. After working with dozens of transformational coaches, I knew Ed's techniques would be helpful; but I had NO idea they would be so powerful. He was able to pinpoint the root of issues I didn't even know were there. Then, he released them FOR me. I barely did anything, but I felt everything. It was like spiritual surgery! I'm still in shock, although I feel 100x better about my life. But unlike most modalities, I know in my heart that this release is permanent. I feel like a new man!"

~ Adam Lipinski, CEO
Abundance Unlimited, LLC

I dedicate this book to all the adversities I've experienced in my life that have ultimately guided me to profound realizations of possibilities, blessings, and healing—far beyond what I could have imagined or hoped for.

I also dedicate it to all the clients who have pushed me to look for continually greater levels of breakthroughs by bringing me tougher and tougher challenges. I bless and love you all.

FREE - BONUS TRAINING

This book includes a video MasterClass about the factors involved in *Answering Your Wake-Up Call.*

Because it is much easier to change the video than edit and publish the book, the MasterClass is likely to contain additional material.

Get it now at: www.LifesNewGame.com/masterclass

Contents

Acknowledgments

While this is not the longest book I've written, it may be the most important. That's especially significant considering that the book I co-authored with Doug Krug, *Enlightened Leadership: Getting to the Heart of Change*, sold some 295,000 copies and has helped thousands of people.

Answering Your Wake-Up Call began at a low point in my life, but it was completed at the highest point of my life—so far.

The book would never have happened if scores of clients, most of them experiencing a midlife detour, hadn't had faith in me. I cannot name them all, so I'll focus on a few who got this work kick-started and who continued to trust me even when some of their early results were less than extraordinary. By putting their trust in me, these people led me to more and more breakthroughs and realizations about what it takes to be all we came here to be.

At my very first public presentation of this work as it existed in January 2015, at a conference in Phoenix, nine people approached me and insisted on working with me. Moreover, as several months of work with them were coming to an end, seven of them insisted on being certified to do this work for their clients. Gayle Abbott, Phil Bristol, Jack Elson, Dan Grobarchik, Tom Lemanski, Tricia Neves, and Elizabeth Weihmiller: I am indebted to you for your trust and confidence in me and in this work. Blessings!

It's amazing how smoothly life goes when you're connected and in tune with the universe. I was inspired to move to St. Petersburg, Florida, in June of 2016. In my mind, I was moving away from the masculine energy of the Colorado mountains to the feminine, nurturing energy of the water. It turns out that was only one reason why I moved. My soulmate, Mary Reid, was there, and I reconnected with Mary, whom I had known for some forty-two years. Mary, you have been a godsend, as you tirelessly support me, are the second guinea pig—after myself—for new realizations, and provide a level of love I've seldom known, or allowed, before.

To all the people from Leon Smith Publishing who have guided me, thank you for your tireless prodding, questions, love, and support.

Last, I do want to say that every one of my clients has provided new learnings that have kept this work accelerating to reach the power and effectiveness it has upon this writing. And it just keeps going. Every client adds to it. Thank you. You bless me beyond words. Touch base with me. Let me know how you're doing. One of my greatest joys is when my clients become my friends.

Introduction

Answering Your Wake-Up Call was written to inspire you to become all you are intended to be, to help you make the difference you were born to make. However, it's not as much about inspiration as it is a revelation that you were born into this life to make a significant impact on the world—even more than you have accomplished so far. And—this part is very important—it's about what you need to do to unleash the essence of who you really are—that part of you that has peeked out from time to time, but has not yet been fully revealed.

This book provides a whole new perspective on the concept of an optimal life and gives you a practical way to attain it. I call this new system *Life's New Game*™. I think of life as a wonderful game, a game of learning, growing, experiencing, and contributing. Let's take the self-imposed limits off the game so we can charge ahead freely.

That's what *Answering Your Wake-Up Call* is all about.

It is about addressing, head-on, the challenges that are staring you in the face. It is about waking up to ideas you've never considered before, to ideas you have shunned because they don't fit your limited belief system. Don't be offended by that statement. We all have limiting beliefs. It is when you treat your *beliefs* as if they are *facts* that they become erroneous and debilitating.

If you picked up this book, I'm betting you're having some kind of mid-life detour, downturn, or flat-out crisis. I've had this same kind of crisis. I'm here to ask you to look at it from a different perspective:

Could it be that you are experiencing a wake-up call?

Do you find yourself wondering:

- *What's missing?*

- *Why is this happening to me?*

- *What am I supposed to do?*

Have you ignored some prodding from the universe in the past?

Is this one a bit tougher, a lot tougher?

If you're anything like me, you've already blown off multiple wake-up calls—smaller ones that were like little taps on the shoulder, nudges, as well as some bigger ones that were like screams, or maybe even a slap on the face.

I caution you not to ignore this one.

If you stick to your narrow, limited beliefs—as I did for so long—you will stay dormant, sleeping through your life. You can use your wake-up call as an opportunity to grow, to thrive, to wake up to new possibilities, to make a difference, and to love your life.

This book's intent is to provide some guidance for you as you awaken. It is intended to help you sort through what your real issues might be, and figure out what to do about them, not only to get you back on track, but to accelerate your life to fulfill your purpose. You might not realize it yet, but there is a specific reason you are alive at this time. Without your contribution, we will all be missing out on something that only you can provide. Part of answering the wake-up call is determining what that is. When you discover it, a life of meaning, joy, and fulfillment can begin. Your life can be extraordinary.

Yes, you've probably already contributed to humankind in numerous ways, but there is more for you to do, or you wouldn't be reading this.

What I hope you'll gain first from this book is a sense of why you're having a wake-up call. After that, you'll need to figure out what to do to answer the call so it can take you to a higher perspective from which you can see who you were born to be. When you follow this lead and become that person, you will accelerate into a life of love, service, and prosperity.

I hope to help you answer the following questions for yourself while reading this work:

- *What are the underlying reasons this wake-up call is happening to me?*

- *What are the best options for me in addressing them?*

- *Why hasn't the personal development work I've already done resolved my issues?*

- *What remains for me to do?*

It is my honor to serve as your guide by sharing what I learned from answering my wake-up call.

Blessings on your journey.

CHAPTER ONE

Your Challenges Are Not What They Appear to Be

We cannot solve our problems with the same thinking we used when we created them.

~ widely attributed to Albert Einstein

The universe has funny ways of getting our attention. I should say *peculiar,* because they're usually not funny at all.

They might look like:

- Stress and overwhelm
- Financial challenges
- Relationship issues
- Wellness issues

I think of them as wake-up calls now, but I haven't always responded to them by waking up. Hopefully, you don't ignore them the way I have so many times; they tend to push you harder and harder until you do address them.

The good news is there are solutions to nearly all wake-up calls. I say *nearly* because if you put off addressing them for too long, there might be a point of no return. Business failure, divorce, serious accidents, and illness are some possible consequences.

Over the years, I have experienced some of these consequences due to my own failure to respond to the prodding of the universe.

Are you getting the message that the challenges and struggles you're facing might not be what they appear to be?

THE OUTER GAME AND THE INNER GAME

There are two parts to the Game of Life. There is the Outer Game, or the Hard Part, which is about what you do. And there is the Inner Game, the Soft Part, which is about who you are.

The challenges, limitations, and struggles you are encountering are not likely what they appear to be. Oh, yes, they are very real—but they are probably not caused by what you think.

The Outer Game: What You Do

The Outer Game includes the processes, the procedures, the tools, and the systems you use. It also includes the talents you have, your personal strengths, and your competencies. The Outer Game is *what you do*. This is arguably the most time-consuming part of the game. It is what most of us would consider *the hard part* because it is the active part of the game. You actively apply all these tools and strengths as you do your work and live your life.

The Outer Game is all about the myriad tasks you need to do to become successful. For example, if you are an entrepreneur or you own your own business, the Outer Game includes the many aspects of marketing, sales, the delivery of services or products, the creation of products and services, all the things you must do to make sure customers or clients are delighted, and the administrative work you must do. The list goes on and on.

The Inner Game: Who You Are

Meanwhile, what may be drastically interrupting the flow of the outer game, and thus, impacting your results, is your *Inner Game*. The Inner Game is formed by the fears and worries you have, like the worry that you have it all wrong, your uncertainty about making decisions, and the nagging feeling you are not crystal clear on where your focus should be.

Those fears, those worries, as well as your lack of focus and clarity, are dependent on personal issues—a *soft* part of you that you may not have had to deal with for a long time. Life may have worked reasonably well for you for years. You may have been employed in a corporate environment without having much of a personal investment—if you weren't personally responsible for the bottom line. You may have been frustrated all day long but were able to go home and recover each night before going back into that frustrating environment again. Even if you are someone who did create your own successful business, you may have been able to pull that off without ever dealing with your own deeper issues.

But now something has changed, and you can feel it. Something isn't working the way it has in the past. Something has changed, and you don't know what.

The Inner Game is personal. It consists of your ideas, your fears, your energy, your clarity, your focus, your attitudes, your struggles. It is the source of your motivation while you conduct the Outer Game. While the Outer Game is about *what you do,* the Inner Game is about *who you are.*

What you need to know is this: the Inner Game has a *huge* impact on the quality of the work you do in the Outer Game.

If you are consumed with fear about whether you are doing the right thing, you may be stymied in the workings of your Outer Game. You might be stuck, without understanding why. This leads to confusion and frustration. The Inner Game is impacted by your limiting beliefs and debilitating emotions, many of which you may not even know you have. The only way to find clarity is to get to the bottom of who you really are.

Are you feeling frustrated and confused?

If so, the universe is nudging you to tell you that it is time to resolve the deep, personal issues that are blocking your next level of success. This work is about getting to who you really are.

Who are you?

You are a brilliant, amazing, and divine being who is here for a purpose.

After Michelangelo unveiled his brilliant statue of David, a seventeen-foot masterpiece, it is said that someone asked him how in the world he had discovered that masterpiece within a huge chunk of marble.

Michelangelo is said to have responded something like, "It was easy. I just removed the pieces of marble that did not fit."

You are the statue of David at the beginning. Think of yourself this way, and you'll see exactly what this work is about for you—*it's about removing the pieces that don't fit.*

When you remove those pieces that do not fit, your brilliance will be allowed to shine, your knowing will come out, your clarity, your focus, your motivation, your energy, your creativity—everything will work when you are truly who you came here to be. And that is what the work of *Life's New Game* is all about.

Taking Right Action

There is a general belief that the most important thing we need to do is *take action*. I've heard consultants and coaches say that over and over. I agree—almost. There is one problem with this idea, however.

The most important thing is not simply taking action, but taking the *right* action.

Taking the right action is highly dependent upon the Inner Game. While the Outer Game is where we spend most of our time, the Inner Game really makes a difference in our effectiveness. When you are worried, when you are preoccupied with fear of failure, you may be so afraid of taking the wrong action that you lose focus and get stuck, which causes your effectiveness to go rapidly downhill.

However, when you are clear-minded about your Inner Game, you know what the right actions are. Then, it becomes easy to do the tasks in the Outer Game. What makes everything difficult in the first place is lack of clarity on what is the right thing to do. When the soft part is handled, the hard part becomes clear. You will find more motivation and energy. Tasks are no longer drudgery and are easily accomplished once we know the right action. And that is the importance and value of the Inner Game.

The bottom line: to be in the top 10–20 percent of successful entrepreneurs and business people, you need to deal effectively with the Inner Game.

Although it seems like most of our time and energy is put into the Outer Game, the Inner Game cannot be ignored. Finding personal clarity is vital for success, and this book will show you some ways to get there.

THE CHALLENGES WE SEE OVER AND OVER

If this book is making sense to you, it is probably because you can relate to some of the challenges we are discussing. In our work, we've found that so many of our entrepreneurial and corporate clients have experienced these same challenges. In this section, we will talk more about them.

After working with scores of entrepreneurs, we realized that all their important issues—overwhelm and stress, cash and cashflow problems, relationship and wellness issues—have a similar origin. All these issues get back to the personal issues, soft issues that haven't been adequately dealt with.

The wake-up call we've been talking about is a message for you from the universe, and it is speaking to you about this idea.

It tells us: *You know, there are some things you need to do before you can truly be the inspired person you were intended to be and make the difference you want to make. And you need to deal with these. They are not going away on their own. These are personal issues. These are the soft issues. You must address them before you can succeed and accomplish what you came here to accomplish and make the difference you are here to make. It is time to deal with those issues.*

One key to being effective in all our jobs is focus. You cannot focus effectively if you are stressed and overwhelmed with everything there is to do. Everything looks impossible when you are in that mode. The only reason you are in that mode is because you have limiting beliefs and debilitating emotions that have been there for years and years.

We have all had emotional traumas that are coming up to scream as we have new challenges we have not faced before.

Maybe you've never worked for yourself before. Maybe you've never had to do all these tasks, and now you must do them all. Naturally, the added stress may trigger the emotional baggage you have.

Stress Prevents Effective Focus

Stress is a primary issue for anyone. There is so much to do as a business person or entrepreneur and for so many people, the responsibilities can quickly become overwhelming. If you started in the corporate world, you may have become accustomed to a corporate system in which you did your piece and then handed off the work to someone else. As an entrepreneur, however, you might need to do it all yourself. In addition, in the corporate world, it is likely you never had to deal with the personal issues we have been talking about.

It is not surprising that we find many entrepreneurs are struggling. If you are struggling, you are probably having a difficult time staying focused and working effectively. You are probably having a difficult time deciding what the right actions are and how to set your priorities for those actions.

Cash and Cashflow Issues Limit Our Ability to Invest in Ourselves

The entrepreneurs who come to us for help often have cash and cashflow issues. It makes sense. I mean, let's face it, we human beings tend to wait until we are confronted with a hard issue before we start addressing the limitations that are facing us. Remember, while cash and cashflow issues are hard issues that are part of the Outer Game, what is causing them is a soft issue, which is part of your Inner Game.

If you are a person newly in business for yourself, you may never have had to deal with your personal issues, your emotions, your limiting beliefs—at least not as thoroughly as life is now demanding. It's a new game now. And even though cash and cashflow is a hard issue, inevitably it is a wake-up call to look at personal issues you need to deal with.

One of the important things we need to do as entrepreneurs is invest in ourselves and invest in our businesses. The challenge with that is that it needs to happen at the same time we are struggling to bring cash into our business. It often seems like the flow of cash is more out than in, and that is a real problem for us. But it all goes back to issues we have never dealt with before.

When you find the clarity you need, you will know what you need to focus on today, tomorrow, and next week. You can turn confusion into clarity, separate out all the things you need to do, and understand exactly when you need to do them.

When you find clarity through your personal growth—when you are coming from who you truly are—your priorities will become clear. You will know what you need to do today and what can wait until later. And when tomorrow comes, you will have a plan, so you will not be overwhelmed with dozens of things that need to get done.

As you clear the baggage and you come closer and closer to knowing who you are, your intuition will kick in, and you will know what to do.

And when you know what to do, you know what?

The doing part is easy. I bet you can relate to that.

Relationship and Wellness Issues Take an Emotional Toll

Sometimes, relationship issues develop because of all the challenges in your business. Cash and cashflow issues, for instance, can put a strain on a relationship. When you are stressed and overwhelmed, you might not be giving your relationships the kind of attention they need. At the same time, when you are stressed and overwhelmed, wellness issues often come up, and health issues have an impact on our relationships as well. As a further complication, the wellness issues and relationship issues distract you and squelch your creativity, the creativity you need for the Outer Game, to do the processes, the procedures, to do the right thing for your business.

Now this is a real challenge; these issues are all intermixed. You cannot separate stress from relationship issues or from wellness issues. Problems with our health are often created by stress and indeed, when we have stress, it is going to put a strain on our relationships.

And when you have a strain on your health and relationships, guess what that is going to do?

Put a stress on your business.

So, it is all wrapped together in one package.

If you are a new entrepreneur, you are trying to do something that is important to you. You want to succeed; you want to take care of your own needs and that of your family. At this stage in your life, maybe you also want to make a bigger difference; perhaps you want to leave a legacy. Maybe there is something you want to do that you know can make a difference on the planet; you may know something that can possibly help a lot of people.

And yet, you are struggling. So much is in the way. All these problems—the cashflow, the stress, the overload, the relationship issues—and now your knee is starting to hurt. It hurts to walk and that pain gets your attention. It blocks your creativity and clarity. You start to be more uncertain of what to do. And that causes more stress.

And on and on. It just spirals downward.

What do you do?

The key is back in that statue of David. You must find a way to clear everything that is not the real you. And when you do that, watch as your relationships magically heal themselves, and maybe even some of your wellness issues disappear.

HAVING BREAKTHROUGHS BY FOCUSING ON THE INNER GAME

When things aren't going right, we tend to look at our tasks and processes and think: *I must be doing these things wrong.* We look at the Outer Game and wonder what we're doing wrong. However, the key to a breakthrough, in every case I have dealt with, is not in the Outer Game at all; it is in the Inner Game.

Mike

Mike had been successful for decades consulting and coaching sales teams in high-tech companies. He had flourished in every aspect of his life. Life was good.

Recently there had been a downturn in his business, and he couldn't understand why. Cashflow had become a big issue, he was really stressed, somewhat overwhelmed, and that was starting to have an impact on his relationship with his wife. To solve the cash issue, he was seriously considering the sale of his amazing mountain-view home and moving to the family farm in Minnesota. Even though Mike had done a lot of personal and spiritual development work over the years, we worked with him to focus on all the Inner Game aspects, and here is what he said early the following year:

> *I thought that all I wanted to do was hang it all up and live at the family farm in Minnesota, but once you got me so clear on the emotions and beliefs side, while raising my Level of Connection with Divine, I was rejuvenated, to say the least.*
>
> *That's when I realized, Hey, I'm a corporate speaker! The one place in the country that hosts the most corporate events is Las Vegas. Almost every week of the year there are events that would be perfect for my speaking topics. So, we excitedly gave up on the family farm and moved to Nevada and we love it here—in a beautiful area just outside Las Vegas.*

Oh, and one more thing: by the end of February, my business had completely turned around and my entire annual calendar was already 75 percent booked!

Mary

Mary's coaching and training business had been thriving for a couple of decades and when she called me, she said:

Nobody knows this, but I have not been able to pay myself in over a year. We have some serious challenges, and here it is time for me to retire and I could not possibly turn this business over to anyone in this shape. And with all the stress, I'm concerned I might be headed for an expensive divorce.

We worked with her and her team, focusing completely on the Inner Game. During the third week of working with them, she called me and said, "I don't know what you are doing but please keep it up. We are having an epic sales month just in the last few days."

They went on to have 50 percent growth for the year, expected a repeat performance for the following year, and she reported that she had the best vacation she'd had with her husband in many years. All by focusing on the Inner Game—for her and her team.

Phil

Phil called us because he was concerned that he had harmed the relationship with his wife. In this case, he knew he had some emotional issues he needed to deal with, and that was what he wanted us to help him with. Within two weeks, the relationship was turned around, they were happy again, and we continued working with him to address his speaking and consulting business. It had been languishing, but it took off within a few months. And within a year, he had lost sixty pounds. All of this by focusing totally on the Inner Game. The Outer Game took care of itself.

Are you relating to any of these scenarios?

These people did not know what the underlying problems were. They just knew they were not getting the results they wanted.

In the next chapter, I share my personal wake-up call, the huge impact it had on my life, and the realization of the deeper, soft, inner issues that were screaming to be resolved. You'll also start to see the solutions, which might be surprising.

CHAPTER TWO

MY ENLIGHTENING WAKE-UP CALL

The privilege of a lifetime is being who you are.
~ Joseph Campbell, *The Hero's Journey*

YOU HAVE MY ATTENTION!

Wake-up calls come in all different forms. Getting sick was mine. Although it may pale in comparison with experiences some of you may have had, it had a huge impact on me. Regardless of the details of each wake-up message, the message is the same.

In my case, it started with a rash. Over just a few days, the rash spread all over my body. It itched like crazy unless I scratched it. Then it was intensely painful. I immediately started going to doctors, who did blood tests and all kind of other tests.

The results?

This was the message I received from the doctors: *You have an autoimmune disease, but we don't know what it is. All we know is your body is eating itself alive from the inside out.*

The treatment?

They wanted me to take cortisone shots. They made it clear to me that this was not to heal my immune system, but to *calm* my immune system.

I could not believe what I was hearing.

One thing became clear to me: if I took the cortisone shots, I would be calming my immune system simply so that I could live with this condition as I literally withered away to die. Instead of healing my immune system, I would be waiting for my immune system to deteriorate.

That made no sense whatsoever to me. I wanted to heal.

The problem was, I didn't know how to heal an immune system, and it seemed that neither did the medical establishment. After talking to a couple doctors and getting the same message, I started investigating some alternative healing approaches: talking to people, having new experiences, and learning about a variety of different strategies, including one-on-one healing.

I went to see several different kinds of healing practitioners, but nothing was working. The symptoms persisted. I was only sleeping two or three hours a night, and when I did sleep, I wasn't sleeping well. I tossed and turned. I had to move out of the bedroom because my restlessness was keeping my wife awake. I sat up for hours, trying to read, trying to do anything I could think of to distract myself from the itching and the pain. After a few weeks, I was totally exhausted.

A Spiritual Experience I'll Never Forget

Late one night, I was sitting up in bed, my knees up against my chest, arms wrapped around my legs, just rocking, trying to distract myself from the feeling. I could smell the medicinal lotion that was spread all over my body. The tears were coming again.

Was this all there was for me now?

Is this how it would be from now on?

Is this what happens?

You spend your lifetime working, get near retirement age, get sick, and you die?

I could feel the tears roll down my cheeks, and I could taste the saltiness as some of them reached my lips. For the first time in my life, I could understand why someone might consider suicide. I was at the point of complete surrender.

I could hear the sound of my own sobbing. Then, in the depths of my despair, I heard myself yell out.

I must have done it quietly because nobody came running, but I yelled out loudly in my mind: *God, please, please, please help me!*

Then, suddenly, there was quiet. Calmness enfolded me. I had the sense that I was surrounded by a heavenly host of beings, beings who were supportive and comforting. In front of me,

I started seeing scenes from my life flash past on a screen. I could see all the wonderful things that I had done—the trek to every place we had camped, every beach and mountain, all the adventures I'd had with family, friends, and clients. Gosh—climbing Mount Kilimanjaro, trekking to Machu Picchu, flying my private plane all over the United States with my family, and sometimes, to meet clients—scene after scene flashed before my eyes.

I could feel the joy of knowing the impact I was having on clients who were all over the world: China, Europe, Indonesia, Africa. I could see everything I had enjoyed in my life—so many things. It went on and on. I felt myself smiling.

Then I saw, right in the middle of that screen, a picture of my mom.

I knew instantly that here in front of me was the issue I needed to focus on in order to heal. My mom had died when I was two years old. I never really knew her; I just knew this picture. Now I knew that all the emotions around losing my mother so young was the heart of the matter. So many hours and days had been put into all kinds of different therapies, so many that I will not try to name them all.

So many times, I would walk out of the therapeutic situation feeling: *Ah, it is healed. It is finally healed. That felt so good.* But the healing had never been complete, and now I understood that.

Another distinct message was waiting for me that day. It is still there in front of me today. These heavenly beings, it was clear to me, were giving me a choice. I felt that, if I chose to leave, they would make it easy for me. These beings knew that, for the first time in my life, I could understand why someone might want to take their own life because I was so miserable. And I knew it was okay if that was my choice.

Then, as I sat there, still surrounded by their comfort, there was another screen, and on this screen was obviously the future. I was shown that, if I chose to stay, the difference I would make by staying would make what I had done so far in my life—developing 53,000 leaders from sixty-seven different countries—pale in comparison.

Well, that was an exciting proposition!

Suddenly, I felt energized. I opened my eyes, hopped out of bed, ran, full of energy and vigor, downstairs to my home office. I went directly to a shelf and pulled out a workbook that had been sitting there for months.

The Pieces of the Puzzle

The name of the workbook was *Heart Forgiveness*, by Dr. Ed Carlson. I took it back upstairs and started thumbing through the book. As I read, I thought: *Wow, this is about anger with yourself, anger with others, anger with God, and anger with the world; this is all about working through lots of different pieces of emotional issues.*

This workbook seemed perfectly designed for me at this moment. The approach that the author used was based on eighteen-minute guided visualizations. I said to myself: *I can do this.*

The only problem was that, in order to see how I was doing, I would be required to perform energy measurements. Energy measurement has different names—it is sometimes called *muscle testing or applied kinesiology*. It is often used by wellness practitioners to determine what your body needs. I had tried to do it in the past and, frankly, I was not very successful. However, this time, I understood that this was where I was being guided to start my healing. If the process required energy measurement, I decided that I had to learn how to do it.

I started learning about different approaches to energy measurement, using fingers, a pendulum, and other techniques. I honed in on the ones that worked for me. I got better and better at it. And it turns out, energy measurement is one of the best things I have ever learned in my life because it is a powerful tool for decision making. (See the Appendix for more information.)

When I started the work, when I started doing these guided visualizations, I was in a state in which I couldn't do much else. I mean, I could not work, I could not play, I could not sleep— so I figured I might as well be working toward being healed. I started doing the guided visualizations constantly and, within about ten days, I actually started feeling a little bit better. I could tell something good was happening, so I continued the work.

Many Other Perspectives

As I completed this work, I was guided to other activities as well. I was led to different practitioners, including Dr. Bradley

Nelson. His work, which you can read about in his book, *The Emotion Code,* is all about trapped emotions. It's about releasing trapped emotions from the fifty trillion cells of the body.

As I was led to various pieces of the puzzle, I realized some things about myself. I saw that one of my best talents, which I have demonstrated many times in my life, is a special ability to be able to take complex subjects and see them in a simpler light. I also realized that I have the ability to see multiple approaches to the same issue. I can see how little pieces from the essence of each approach can fit together so they can work together. It allows for a kind of synergy. This ability to take many perspectives, see them in a whole different light, and combine them, creates an effective outcome. Using this strategy, the final process is much easier and more effective than each of the elements considered separately. This way of thinking has always been one of my best talents.

I began to see how these processes could be simplified. I saw what was really important—the real essence of the work. I experienced other works along the way that contributed important concepts. I'll highlight the most important ones a bit later.

I began to see how the different approaches were alike, and how they were different. I was seeing and experiencing those various processes in what later seemed to be the perfect order for learning and optimizing.

I Was Feeling Better and Better . . .

By March of 2013, I was feeling better, significantly better. I was intently focused on healing, and although the itching and some other symptoms were still there, I felt stronger, and I had much more energy.

One afternoon, I was surprised to find myself thinking that I wanted to go out to do something. It was the first time in months that I had felt like getting out. I started thinking about what I wanted to do. I looked at my calendar and realized that my friend, Dr. Bill Hines, a prominent ophthalmologist from Denver who is often on the Denver Broncos sideline as a team doctor, would be speaking at a conference that evening. He would be talking about an amazing spiritual experience he'd had after a transformational retreat. I decided to go hear his story.

HOW IMPORTANT IS THIS?

I showed up at the conference just as Bill was getting ready to take the stage. He told an amazing story of going to a retreat overseas and having what he spoke of as "an awakening experience." When he came back home to his medical practice, he was immediately confronted with a difficult eye surgery. Things were not going well; the surgery was going in the wrong direction. He had never experienced this particular situation, and he had no idea what to do.

He told us that he reacted by surrendering to Spirit and asking for help. It was at that moment, after extensive preparation at the retreat, that he sensed a profound awakening. Immediately he was guided, step by step. He started giving orders to his attendants and taking instruments and doing different actions and procedures, things that he had never done before. He was shown exactly how to proceed, and the surgery was an overwhelming success. He walked out of the room knowing that he had been carefully guided through this experience, and he knew that this was due to the fact that he had been awakened at the retreat.

His story was mesmerizing. I knew I'd never had an experience like that, and, while I wasn't sure why, I somehow knew it was important for me to pursue.

Sign Me Up—I Want to Go!

When Bill came off the stage, I was so energized by his talk that I grabbed him immediately and said, "Bill, I want to experience what you experienced, this awakening process."

He said, "Great, can you go April 1st?"

I asked how long the program would be, and he told me they were usually thirty days, but he could get me into a special leadership program that would take six days.

I said, "Hey, I am in!" I did not ask about the fee or anything else; I just said, "I am in."

I immediately started preparing for my journey to Oneness University in India. I was also still working hard to finish up the healing processes that had been my focus over the past six weeks. Much of this work was composed of *clearing* exercises, involving emotional release, the clearing out of old belief systems, and reprogramming. While I was packing, as I was getting on the plane, as I was on the airplane flying to the retreat, I was completing this healing work.

I had a good week overall at the retreat. Some of the experiences were okay, and some of them were extraordinary. I didn't know what to expect from the program. I knew the intention of the workshop was to experience the process of awakening, but I didn't know exactly what that meant.

I can tell you that I recognized the exact moment in which I had the shift I was hoping for. It was on the last afternoon of the last day. I cannot say it was all that significant on the outside—the seas didn't part or anything like that. But I felt this little buzz, a one-second buzz in my brain, and everything changed. All of a sudden, the world looked just a little bit different out in front of me.

It wasn't dramatic. As I started home, I remember thinking to myself: *Wow, if I hadn't known I was here for an experience intended to awaken me, I might never have known that anything had happened.* But I knew. It was subtle, but very clear to me.

When I was flying back home, I noticed a distinct difference in my applied kinesiology work, the energy measurement practice. I had been doing this work for some time now, but for the first time, I could actually measure what I am going to call the *Level of Connection* (LOC) *with Source*.

There are several models of LOC, and I had been trying to measure these levels for a month or so and had not been able to do it. On the way back on the plane, it suddenly locked in, and I was able to measure it consistently.

The people I had been in meditation groups with back home were all below a certain number on the scale of connection with Source, Divine, Creator, or whatever your name for God. I tested the people who had been awakened in my class in India, whose names I remembered, and they were all a little above that number.[1*]

I said, "Oh my goodness; that number on the scale is the point of awakening. And for the first time, I can measure it." This was my first hint that something significant had happened.

I returned home. After getting a few days of rest, I woke up one morning feeling different. Because I was measuring everything now, I was able to measure the fact that, oh my gosh, my energy was *much* higher—100 percent higher.

What else had changed?

My clarity had jumped, my focus ability had surged, and I was having bursts of creativity. The very next day, the same thing happened again, and then again. Four days in a row, I continued to gain enhanced clarity, focus, awareness, creativity, and energy. I was on a roll in my work.

---

1   *There are different scales that measure Level of Connection or Level of Consciousness, but these scales are not relevant to this conversation.

I'm Supposed to Write a Book?

It was during this time that I first got the clear message: *Okay, it is time to go and write a book about this.*

I responded: *No, I don't have time to write a book right now!*

I kept getting that same message to write a book. It actually took me about a month before I finally succumbed to the nudge.

Okay.

I went to our getaway condo in Keystone, Colorado, by myself, and I started writing about my experience. I was energized by the wonderful mountain environment, and all the healing had put me in a remarkable flow state. I wrote wherever it felt right—outdoors when it was warm enough, on the living room couch, at the dining room table, at restaurants and coffee shops in the village. I just allowed it all to flow. I wrote in daylight. I wrote at night. It was an amazing, creative experience.

Five days later, I had finished a 120-page book. One hundred and twenty pages in five days! I had written before. I had written a book that had taken me five years to finish, one that had taken me five months, but never a book in *five days*. I had achieved a flow state that was absolutely amazing.

I finished it at ten o'clock one night. I was exhausted, but very pleased. Then, feeling very grateful for what had happened, I plopped down in bed and fell fast asleep.

Another Kind of Wake-Up Call—at Two in the Morning

It was exactly 2:00 a.m. on the digital clock on the nightstand to the right of my bed when I woke up, knowing something had happened. I did not know what it was, but I knew it was positive and significant. I was immediately wide awake.

You know how sometimes you wake up with a start?

It was not like that. I simply woke up with a feeling of clarity that something good had happened.

I said to myself: *What is it? What happened?*

I immediately started doing my energy measurements on different thoughts. It wasn't long before I got around to testing my illness.

What I realized was that *I had been spontaneously healed of my autoimmune disease.*

A few weeks prior, my condition had finally been diagnosed by a chiropractor—with use of a thousand dollars' worth of blood tests. It involved gluten and lactose intolerance, and I had just begun changing my diet. All of a sudden, it was clear that I no longer had any sensitivity to wheat or to anything else with gluten in it. I also now had no sensitivity to milk, or anything else.

I tested everything on the list I had created over the last few weeks and nothing was showing as an issue! I was stunned and filled with gratitude, and that gratitude leaked out through my tears. Every test result indicated I was not sensitive to gluten or dairy.

Two days later, I tested myself the scary way at Pizza Republica, a restaurant in Greenwood Village, Colorado, by sitting down and, bite by bite, carefully eating, watching, writing, and taking notes. As a final test of gluten sensitivity, I had no problem whatsoever eating half a pizza. Artichoke and pepperoni pizza. It was so good!

The following day, I had one of my favorite things in the world, a milkshake. Again, no problem whatsoever. I had been completely healed.

Why was I so blessed?

Over time, I came to understand that it was because I had more to do to make a difference in the world. I'm not unique in that way. You have more to do as well. You are here for an important purpose. You probably would not be reading this if you were not having your own wake-up call.

Do you get that—is this resonating with you?

MY REVELATION

What was the key to this miraculous healing?

I realized the breakthroughs I had were all experienced since returning from Oneness University. My energy, creativity, focus, awareness, and motivation had skyrocketed within a couple days of returning from the retreat. I had written a 120-

page book in five days. And now, the spontaneous healing of my autoimmune disease had happened!

This Level of Connection with Source/God/Creator/Divine—this Awakening—had to be the key to it all.

Is this the Holy Grail of healing?

I Can't Wait to Talk With Friends from the India Trip

I had connected with about half a dozen people in India, and I wondered how they were doing.

What kind of miracles were they experiencing? I wondered.

I could hardly wait to talk with them about their breakthroughs, and to share mine.

They were scattered from Rhode Island to California. I started calling them. On the first call with David, I blurted out that I wanted to share my miracle and hear about his. That was a mistake because David had nothing good to report. In fact, he said he wished he hadn't spent the time and money to go to India. He hadn't seen any personal value. He was still as stuck as he had been before going.

I was stunned by his response, so I was more cautious when I called John, just asking him if he'd had any kind of breakthroughs. He suggested he felt a bit better, had a little more clarity—but it was nothing like my experience.

Of all the people I called, not one had had the kind of experience that I'd had. I was genuinely surprised and wondered why my experience had been so different.

The Truth Revealed

I thought about what I had done before going to India.

What had I done that perhaps no one else had done, at least, not to the same extent?

Then, it hit me.

In the process of all the personal work I had done in those weeks, I had cleared massive amounts of trapped emotions, like fear of failure, worry, anger, grief, fear of rejection, anxiety, low self-esteem, resentment, unworthiness, rejection, sadness, sorrow, heartache, abandonment, shame, jealousy, overwhelm, humiliation, nervousness, love unreceived, depression, lack of control, and anxiety.

I had spent major amounts of time reprogramming limiting beliefs in order to get myself fully believing in *me*—my mission, my worthiness, my lovability, my reason for being.

None of the people I'd spoken with had done this kind of work. Yes, they had worked on themselves over the years, but not to the depth that I had in the couple of months before the retreat.

That's when I realized it takes *all three* of these elements to achieve major transformation:

- Clearing of trapped emotions

- Reprogramming of limiting beliefs
- Connecting with Source

The reason I was led to go to India became apparent. It was the fastest way to get my attention, to show me the importance of adding the Level of Connection with God, because this had not been addressed by the other work I had done!

What's missing in most personal and spiritual development systems is that they don't transform all three elements. Remember that my spontaneous healing did not occur until the third factor was added. All three elements are required for synergy.

CHAPTER THREE

The Three Factors for Synergy and Miracles

I am realistic—I expect miracles.

~ Wayne Dyer

If you're anything like me, you've spent decades trying to improve yourself in numerous ways. You've worked on those elements that fit in the Outer Game, the more skill-oriented areas, and you've worked on the Inner Game aspects of who you are today. You have probably spent substantial time working on limiting beliefs, and dealing with emotional issues, all with the intent of becoming the most you can be, and to have the happiest, most successful, most fulfilling life you can have. I think you'd say you've grown a lot during that time.

Yet, you're having this wake-up call now. This means that you have more to do.

What you have done was good and important. It simply wasn't enough—no matter how many hours and how much effort and how many tears you shed doing it.

The good news is that the deeper healing is easier than it has ever been, and you don't have to do it alone. We've discovered there are three important parts to opening yourself to the fullness of who you really are—the amazing person you came to be—and we will discuss these further in this chapter.

The following is just an overview, because I'm betting you have had your own experiences with many sources during your lifetime. This overview will help to get us to the real point, the real message.

YOUR BODY: TRAPPED EMOTIONS

This first factor in healing is the Body piece of the puzzle. Over your lifetime, and through multiple generations of DNA that came before, many emotional experiences have accumulated, some big and some small, inside you. Thousands of trapped emotions have been stored in your body over time. They show up in every aspect of our bodies, in our organs, glands, systems, chakras, energy, skeleton, and connective tissues.

Emotions are debilitating in ways that we know, but also can be debilitating in ways—emotionally and physically—that we cannot even imagine. Our negative experiences tend to result in trapped emotions in different parts of our body. It is known that the different organs, glands, and systems of our body attract certain emotions. When you have a particular trauma, emotions about it may show up in your heart; after another trauma, emotions may show up in your kidneys or in other parts of your body.

It is critical for you to release these trapped emotions. As long as they stay trapped, you are literally hurting parts of your body, and until you release the emotions, you will continue to have physical limitations that will likely become worse over time.

Thousands of Emotions Are Trapped in Our Bodies

Until those debilitating emotions are released, we cannot fully be who we came here to be. These emotions keep you from shining in the way you were intended to shine, to blossom, to be that person who is meant to make a difference in some powerful way. You cannot shine as long as you have enormous numbers of these emotions stuck in your body. Dr. Bradley Nelson, in his 2007 book, *The Emotion Code: How to Release Your Trapped Emotions for Abundant Health, Love and Happiness,* identified sixty different trapped emotions that can and do limit your ability to be all that you can be.

Furthermore, you might have the same emotion—resentment, for example—trapped in many different parts of the body. This is one of the reasons that you might have had a great therapeutic, emotion-releasing experience only to have the same emotion show up later.

BREAKTHROUGH

Several years ago, I was struggling in my business. Ed Oakley came to me and said, "Lyman, you have some issues in your life that are holding you back. Do you mind if I clear some of those blockages for you?" I didn't quite understand what he was talking about, but I was open.

I knew three things about Ed. Number one: I knew he was transparent. Number two: I knew that he saw something in me that I did not see in myself. Number three: he shared with me that if I was able to clear these blockages from my life, new worlds that would open up.

I want to share with you what happened. He shared with me some things that I didn't know I was dealing with. I was angry with myself. I had built my business up to half a million dollars just to lose it. I had two failed marriages and I couldn't get it together.

Listen, within two weeks—God as my witness— Ed facilitated the clearing of those blockages, and my life transformed forever. My business for the first time skyrocketed. I'm getting so many clients . . .

~ Lyman Montgomery, CEO,
FocusedDriven.com

How to Approach the Release of Emotions

There are many ways to release these debilitating emotions. The approach that is best for you is dependent upon your available time, resources, and preferences.

Think about it:

- Do you want to release the emotions quickly so that you can get on with the life that you are eager to live?

- Do you have plenty of time to address the issues gradually, one at a time?

- Do you feel compelled to handle the process by yourself?

- What level of investment of time, energy, and money are you willing to make?

These are some of the trade-offs to consider.

Clearing Trapped Emotions Is Critical but Not Sufficient

It is important to realize that releasing the many thousands of emotions trapped throughout your being is a critical part of your personal transformation and well-being. However, although it is necessary, it is not sufficient. While some contend that releasing the trapped emotions is the key to your well-being and bringing out your best, I have found that this is just a piece of the puzzle.

YOUR MIND: THOUGHTS, PATTERNS, AND BELIEFS

The second piece of the puzzle is in your mind. You may have hundreds or thousands of limiting thoughts, patterns, and beliefs. Throughout our lives, as we take different approaches to transform our lives, to make our lives better, we will inevitably discover—gosh—there are just so many limiting beliefs that we did not even realize were there.

An example is the importance of believing in yourself and your mission. It is critical that you believe in yourself and your mission 100 percent in order to be optimally successful at it. You may think that you already do—and this may be true at the conscious level.

But what about deeper levels?

An Overview of Traditional Approaches

One of the traditional approaches to changing patterns of thought is the use of *affirmations*. Affirmations are simply positive statements you say consciously to begin to shift the negative thoughts you might have from life experiences. An affirmation applied over a long period of time can be valuable. Affirmations help us be conscious of what we are saying to ourselves and about ourselves. It is a first step toward trying to change those beliefs that are limiting, the limiting things that you are saying about yourself, your mission, and your life. However, it takes a lot of affirmation to chip away at deep subconscious beliefs. That is a challenge.

Something that I have found to be more effective than affirmations is the use of *afformations*. This approach is presented by Noah St. John in his excellent book, *Afformations: The Miracle of Positive Self-Talk* (Hay House, 2013).

The powerful thing about his process is you ask yourself a question whose answer significantly shifts your mindset.

The process begins by asking yourself a question, particularly an open-ended question like:

- What is special about me?

- What is it about me that is unique and different?

- What are the strengths I have that are going to allow me to make a bigger difference?

Those kinds of questions tend to go much deeper and allow you to shift in that direction over time. The magic of open-ended questions is that they keep processing until the answers are clear in your mind at deeper and deeper levels. Though it is going to take a significant amount of time and many effective questions, I recommend doing this until you naturally think of yourself, others, and the world in this forward-focused way of thinking, regardless of your greater strategy for transformation.

When you ask yourself these open-ended questions, your mind doesn't stop processing them until it receives answers. So, imagine how you'll feel differently about yourself when you start gaining clarity about: *What is special about me?* Do you see the value in that?

Other therapies, like *Theta Healing*, hypnosis, *Psych-K*, and neuro-linguistic programming, can be effective in reprogramming our limiting beliefs once they are identified. Of course, identifying them is part of the challenge, because frankly, there are many to discover in all of us!

The Importance of the Subconscious Mind and Beyond

These beliefs are not only conscious beliefs, but include subconscious and unconscious. It is relatively easy for us to know the conscious ones, but the other ones are often hidden from us.

I've known many people who have performed decades of affirmations and other belief work and still don't believe in themselves completely. If you are one of these people and you still have a little doubt, that doubt will hold you back. For you to contribute what you want and be who you want to be, there is no compromise on this one. One hundred percent belief in yourself and in your mission is required.

If I asked you if you believe in yourself and your mission, I'll bet you'd say yes quite strongly. I have no doubt that would be true—*at the conscious level.*

From the excellent work of Vianna Stibal, *Theta Healing: Introducing an Extraordinary Energy-Healing Modality* (Rolling Thunder Publishing, 2010), as well as her other books, we realize our beliefs are found on many levels, not only on what she calls the *core* level, which is what we've been discussing, but also on a *genetic* level, a *history level*—possibly including past lives—and a *soul* level. There are potentially additional levels as well.

I have found that traditional approaches to shifting beliefs, like affirmations, and even more advanced modalities, while valuable, do not touch some of these other levels.

Are you starting to feel like this is an impossible task?

Hang in there! Help is coming.

BREAKTHROUGH

I gave the speech of my life . . . and sold over $17,000 in product sales.

Several years ago, I had a major setback. It happened the night before a major speaking engagement. My bank had dropped my line of credit without warning or cause. I had been with them for over a decade and worried that my business was in jeopardy. I was so distraught, I did not think I could do the speech. After talking to Ed for only ten minutes, he reminded me how to clear those negative emotions with the Enlightened Transformation process. I did and then gave the speech of my life the next morning. I connected so well with the audience, I sold over $17,000 in product sales—an all-time record at that time.

~ Ed T., Toastmasters World Champion speaker

Reprogramming Your Limiting Beliefs Is Critical, but Not Sufficient

While reprogramming thousands of limiting beliefs at all the levels involved is a requirement for unleashing the best you, this alone is not sufficient for bringing out the real you. Just as it was not sufficient to release all the trapped emotions, it is not sufficient just to reprogram beliefs, even at all levels.

YOUR SPIRIT: CONNECTION WITH SOURCE

For you to be fully who you are here to be, the third element—connection with the Creator of All That Is, God, Source, Divine, Yahweh, Jesus, Buddha, however you see it—is critical. This was the factor, that when added to my reprogramming of hundreds of limiting beliefs and clearing thousands of trapped emotions—including abandonment, anger, resentment, and many beliefs about my mom dying when I was two years old—led to my spontaneous healing. And no, I cannot predict resolution of health and wellness issues for you. Sorry! I'm not a healthcare professional of any kind.

Connection with Source and Consciousness

Some people have addressed this part of who they are by meditating, seriously meditating, sometimes for decades, to try to enhance their connection with Source. I honor that. I admire that commitment. I tried to meditate for many years but, frankly, I tended to fall asleep, and my lack of patience led to frustration. However, after I achieved the awakening at the retreat in India, my meditations became powerful, easy, and an important part of my life.

Can you relate to any of this?

Oneness University is just one option for enhancing your Connection with Divine; we'll look at another in the next chapter. Oneness University offers weeklong to month-long events in India, and numerous events throughout North America and other parts of the world.

BREAKTHROUGH

She SMILES when I enter the room!

I took my wife to dinner Monday night. She had a tough day. And since I've become more aware and empathetic, I noticed and asked her out. She accepted.

At the end of dinner, with little preface or framing, I asked: "Have you noticed anything different about me since starting Life's New Game?"

Her answer surprised me. She enthusiastically shared a list of noticeable changes, including the following:

"You're happier. Less stressed.

"You're easier to work with, to be around.

"You've been voluntarily taking on a lot of little home improvement projects.

"You actually bought flowers for Valentine's Day; I was floored.

"I feel better—not apprehensive—when you enter the room."

Apparently, there's more to this New Game than sleeping better, having a great vacation, and predicting basketball results. Not that there's anything wrong with those.

~Ted, CEO Coach

Ted also later told us that his business was the best it had ever been.

Connection with Source Is Critical but Also Requires the Other Two Elements

Since my spontaneous healing, it has been confirmed numerous times that to be all that you were born to be requires all three of these elements. You must:

1. Release the thousands of trapped emotions from the fifty trillion cells of your body.

2. Reprogram the thousands of limiting conscious, subconscious, and unconscious beliefs at the core, genetic, history, and soul levels.

3. Raise your Connection with Source to breakthrough levels.

It does not matter how you accomplish these three tasks. You can take one approach to number one. You can take another approach to number two, another approach to do number three. But all three are required to release your full brilliance, the amazing *you* that is here for a divine purpose.

Emotions are important. Beliefs are important. Level of Connection is important. However, it is the synergy between these three factors that will enable you to accomplish your purpose.

If all you transform is two of the three factors, you get 1 + 1 = 2, but when all three are combined, the results are far, far more than 1 + 1 + 1 = 3! It's more like 1 + 1 + 1 = 30. Miracles can and do happen.

CHAPTER FOUR

Transformation Made Simple AND Easy

I would not give a fig for the simplicity this side of complexity, but I would give my life for the simplicity on the other side of complexity.
~ attributed to Oliver Wendell Holmes

My very best talent is an ability to look at numerous perspectives, capture the pieces that are important from each, determine their true essence, then recombine them in a different way to create a simpler way to accomplish results—a way that is more effective than the sum of the parts. That's what *synergy* is.

Synergy is miraculous—by definition, it produces much more than the sum of the parts. This applies to your effectiveness, the results you are trying to accomplish, and the time required to do it.

BREAKTHROUGH

This impacted the whole family.

We want to tell you about our experience in working with Ed. He used his Enlightened Transformation process to in-tune my husband and me along with our daughter, who happens to be eight years old and just did a keynote address in front of two thousand people, about how young entrepreneurs are going to change the world. We have seen actual physical changes in this reality based on working with Ed.

We also saw an increase in the cashflow from both of our businesses since we started with Life's New Game. We have seen huge results. In the three-and-a-half months since working with Ed, we have tripled our monthly cashflow.

~ Tonya Dawn Recla, Deputy Director,
Super Power Experts
~ Justin Recla, Operations Officer,
Clear Business Directory and
Cryptobit Verified Crypto Currency Due Diligence
SuperPowerExperts.com, ClearBusinessDirectory.com

FACTORS IN MY LEARNING

As previously mentioned, I was guided to numerous approaches for each of the different aspects of my healing. I want to honor each of them for the specific pieces they contributed to my recovery, breakthroughs, and new levels of thriving. While this list is not complete, they were all important. I share them with you to provide options for your consideration.

Key Contributors

Dr. Ed Carlson's exceptional works, especially *Heart Forgiveness* and *Core Health*, showed me that an 18-minute guided visualization process could gradually clear emotional and belief issues when they are specifically addressed in the process. Over time, I discovered how to take the essence of the approach and create a unique Divine request that is effective in less time.

Dr. Bradley Nelson's amazing book, *The Emotion Code*, and his *Body Code* program showed me that there are many different emotional traumas trapped in every aspect of our bodies—systems, organs, glands, chakras. Over sixty different debilitating emotions, psychic traumas, and other kinds of issues may be trapped in the fifty trillion cells of our bodies. I gradually realized how to clear them by modifying the process I had already created. I didn't have to relive the trauma that some approaches require, and working with both beliefs and with different kinds of emotional challenges at the same time was a big time saver.

Through the work I did with Oneness University, I discovered how to raise Level of Connection with Source. It was far more important than I realized at the time, as you have already discovered by hearing my spontaneous healing story.

Through working with many clients, I have realized over time how to integrate that into my simple prayer process that now raises Level of Connection every time it is used. Learning how to measure the Level of Connection and Consciousness was also important for me; they help me understand what limitations an individual might be facing.

I learned from numerous sources, including my work with *Enlightened Leadership,* that enhancing our empowering aspects—for both beliefs and emotions—is also important on the path to becoming all that we were intended to be. Accordingly, the work I found so effective in working with thousands of leaders is included in the advanced processes that have evolved. Further enhancing your better strengths is as important as removing your limitations.

Does this make sense to you?

Vianna Stibal's deep *Theta Healing* work taught me that there were issues not only at the *core* level, which other modalities were already addressing, but also at the *genetic, history,* and *soul* levels. This was another breakthrough in effectiveness as I discovered I could identify genetic, history, and soul levels in my process, and each of those levels clear a measurable amount each time the process is used. This takes the work much deeper in the advanced work we do for clients.

Meanwhile, as my research continued, I discovered my own breakthrough perspectives, more and more limiting beliefs, and emotional traumas that could be released without having to identify each one. No longer do we have to identify every emotional trauma and every limiting belief to release and reprogram them. No longer do we have to relive the emotional pain to release it.

Do you see the value in that?

The Bathtub Analogy

I like the bathtub analogy. Imagine a bathtub full of oily, grimy, dirty water that represents the trapped emotions and the limiting beliefs in our body systems.

Healing or correcting these issues often involves identifying a particular trauma. For example, consider the trauma of my mother's death. That is waaaaaaay down in the bathtub, near the bottom because it was early in my life.

Many approaches would require identifying the issue near the bottom of the tub, re-experiencing the pain in some cases, and using various approaches to release it. That's analogous to taking a straw and reaching down into the dirty water to capture that one little issue, then pulling it out and releasing it outside the tub.

But what happens to the level of grimy water in the tub when a straw's worth of emotion is released?

Not much! It's still pretty full of yucky stuff (that's your body, you know).

You often feel it when emotions release, which definitely has some value. I know because I've done that one numerous times during the earlier years of my life in different ways and felt it most every time.

What's wrong with that picture? If I feel it every time, then it was never fully released!

And that's just one issue or situation.

You Don't Have to Identify Every Little Issue

Over time, I have been guided to a new strategy, a way of clearing issues by peeling away layers. If you use this technique, it isn't necessary to identify and process every single issue. We can remove the uppermost layer of emotions and massively release beliefs by continuing to add to the list of beliefs that is reprogrammed more and more each time it is used. After releasing that layer, the advanced process moves to the next layer and then to the next. This greatly diminishes the time needed to release and reprogram decades of trapped emotions and limiting beliefs.

Over the last six years, I've received more and more clarity regarding what our system needed to address to fulfill its mission of removing all the pieces that are not you while enhancing the positive traits that optimize who you are.

BREAKTHROUGH

Dave came to me because he had been impacted by Enlightened Leadership training years before and wanted to know if he could teach it within his own communities. I said yes under one condition: that he go through the Advanced Level of Life's New Game so he could be the leader he wanted to teach about. He agreed and started the process.

The following week, he sent me an email. After the first week, he had softened so much that it shifted the relationship with his teenage daughter, and he experienced her shifting for the better, too. He was amazed.

Then, after another few weeks—during which he had several meetings with top managers—with him coming from this new place, the CEO called him in to talk with him about becoming Chief Engineer, a post that he had wanted for years. At the end of that week, if that wasn't enough, he got an unsolicited call from another substantial company who wanted to talk with him about a Chief Engineer role there. And that was just the first few weeks. He is now the Chief Engineer of a significant company and working just blocks from his home.

~ Dave B., Chief Engineer

DAILY DEVELOP™ SYSTEM

What has evolved from all this preparation is *Life's New Game's Daily DEVELOP* system. This system is intended to remove your disabling and disempowering issues gradually, while enhancing your empowering issues to move you closer and closer to your ideal self, so that you can live and serve from the brilliance of who you really are.

The Seven Factors

Let's define the seven components of the Daily DEVELOP system:

D - Decrease your emotional baggage (daily)

E - Erase your limiting beliefs (daily)

V - Voice your gratitude (daily)

E - Enhance empowering beliefs and emotions (daily)

L - Lift your Connection with your Creator (daily)

O - Observe the shifts you're having (daily)

P - Praise God for the upgrades (daily)

It is important to note that the *Daily DEVELOP* system works with any approaches that deal with all the individual pieces or any combination of approaches that address them all. You don't have to use our process. You can address the different factors with numerous methods. Just be sure to release, reprogram, or enhance them all—Body, Mind and Spirit! In fact, we've already identified some excellent resources and approaches in this chapter. What is important is that you address them all methodically, effectively, and thoroughly. How you choose to do it is not as important as your *choice* to do it. You should choose your approaches based on your needs regarding time, resources, and preferences.

The *VOP* of DEVELOP: The Three Quick, Easy Steps

Note that three of the elements are quick and easy, regardless of the approach you take:

- **Voice** your gratitude.
- **Observe** your shifts.
- **Praise** God for the upgrades.

These are important practices you should be doing every day, regardless of the approach you take for the tougher factors. Gratitude is a very important and powerful part of healing.

The *DEEL* of DEVELOP: The Big Four

These are the big four issues for unleashing the optimum *you*. Addressing these issues can vary dramatically in time, effort, cost, and pain involved.

- **Decrease** your emotional baggage. Trapped emotions limit you in many ways.

- **Erase** your limiting beliefs at all levels. Limiting beliefs keep you from being all that you can and should be.

- **Enhance** your empowering beliefs and emotions at all levels. These factors are your rocket fuel once you've removed your restraints.

- **Lift** your Connection with Source/Divine/God. This enhances your awareness, focus, clarity, motivation, energy, and creativity.

The last element is so important, yet few approaches to personal transformation address your connection with Source at all. If they say they do, look for proof, because many practitioners think they are doing this important piece of the work, but are not. Most are simply assuming their important work automatically enhances connection. Very few processes actually do.

BREAKTHROUGH

Early on, I felt like there was a veil that was lifted. A veil of confusion or overwhelm or fear. And that was lifted very early, which allowed me to keep moving forward even though I was in my busiest time of the year. And one of the most intense weeks I've had, as far as business goes. I don't usually do that with five new keynotes in three days in three cities. Not just new material: new content, new speech, new PowerPoint, new marketing things. Really jumping out of my comfort zone. And I feel like I was really supported here.

> *Even after only three hours of sleep last night, I gave the best speech of my career. Not because it was perfect, but because I connected in an amazing way.*
>
> ~ Diane S., speaker, author, coach, nurse

HOW MUCH TIME DO YOU HAVE?

Time issues and flexibility vary significantly from person to person. How much time do you have?

If You Have Plenty of Time . . .

If you're not spending a lot of your day working, or busy with important projects, you are fortunate. You have many options, including the ones we have identified for you earlier in this work. Just make sure you combine them in a way that measurably addresses Body, Mind, and Spirit.

If Time Is a Critical Factor for You . . .

If you're a busy coach, consultant, leader, or entrepreneur, time may be one of your greatest challenges. It is you for whom *Life's New Game* was ideally designed, because I recognized in my own work-life that I had personal issues to resolve, but I found it hard to find the time to address them, much less the time to experiment with numerous approaches. I have found this to be the case for many people and companies with which I have worked.

The approach of *Life's New Game* is developed for the busy person who wants to optimize their life but doesn't have much spare time to do it. Interestingly, the approach also can work well in communities of people. It has worked well for small businesses and for larger organizations where consultants and coaches have used the heart of *Life's New Game, Enlightened Transformation.*

The Enlightened Transformation Process

The heart of our *Daily DEVELOP* system is our process called *Enlightened Transformation,* which comes in several versions—depending on the person's current stage of personal development. The Primary version gets all three factors improving gradually, and the Advanced version cranks up the depth and speed to progress, as well as dealing with some special situations.

Enlightened Transformation is a proven Divine request, or a prayer, for transforming a layer at a time of the different aspects of the *Daily DEVELOP* system. The process addresses everything in the DEVELOP acronym at the same time, layer by layer, clearing by clearing, enhancement by enhancement, increasing Level of Connection with your Creator every time it is used.

Do you get the significance of this?

When I first developed a working prayer, or abbreviated visualization, it worked to support my healing and breakthroughs, but it took a lot of time—about fifteen minutes each time it was used. I sensed it needed to be done at least twice a day, so, early on, we recommended thirty to forty-five minutes a day or more. While the healing was well worth that time investment, it did not work well for the person fully engaged with work and other responsibilities.

Over the last five years, what started as this crude, lengthy process has been refined many times. We set out to improve it so that it could take less time, yet clear more and more issues on different levels, while enhancing empowering aspects and raising Level of Connection with Divine every time it is used.[2]*

A major breakthrough allowed us to cut it to less than ten minutes each time, so doing the process twice a day only took the time of a typical meditation, about twenty minutes per day. That was an improvement.

I could have stopped there, but I also wanted to add some additional experiences to *Life's New Game*—such as a brief video every week or two, a ten-minute exercise from time to time, an occasional educational email. I also wanted to provide some group or private calls for specialized work. All this took the client's time, so I continued working to improve the effectiveness of the process while decreasing the time required.

Does that make sense?

Currently, the *Life's New Game* program consists of periodic emails, videos, assignments and calls, and twice-a-day use of

---

2   * I cannot overemphasize that this is true only for people who have read this book. Reading the book will provide a learning experience that will function as an initiation for use of this process.

the *Enlightened Transformation* process. All of this requires less than 7 minutes a day on average, and that's when you're using our optional advanced system, which is more extensive. The Primary system takes less than one minute each time you use it, and we suggest using it several times per day.

We continue to enhance the process and system with each new discovery, while adding to our extensive clearing list, which currently has tens of thousands of emotional and belief factors to clear or enhance. Every time the *Enlightened Transformation* process is used, each and every one of those factors is diminished or enhanced until it has reached the point of being ideal for the individual, and this point varies with the needs of the individual.

For example, some issues will be resolved with just a few uses of the process. Some might take dozens of times. I used our advanced process recently to reduce my addiction to sugar. It took dozens of times, and it worked. That ended my daily ice cream—both the consumption and the desire.

I believe that each of us has a mission to do while we're here. Your job is to become all you were intended to be in Body, Mind, and Spirit and make the difference you were intended to make. How you get there is irrelevant. It's your choice.

Blessings for finding the right approach for you!

CHAPTER FIVE

The Secret Sauce

Simplicity is the ultimate sophistication.
~ attributed to Leonardo da Vinci

WHAT'S THE SECRET SAUCE IN ALL THIS?

Let me describe our *Enlightened Transformation Primary Process*. It is a declaration, prayer, or request for what we want. It addresses, at a Primary level, all three enhancements we've been discussing.

The Three Factors: Body, Mind, and Spirit

- Body—Emotions:

Enlightened Transformation releases more and more trapped emotions from all the systems, organs, glands and chakras of our bodies each time it is used. Although I had cleared my abandonment and anger issues about Mom to some extent in the many therapeutic approaches I had tried, I had not cleared them thoroughly at all levels and all timeframes until I developed a more thorough process.

- Mind—Beliefs:

Enlightened Transformation reprograms thousands of limiting beliefs, a little at a time, each time the process is used. It takes less than a minute to initiate, and typically three to ten minutes to fully process. All you need to do is start the process and go about your business. It also enhances empowering beliefs at the same time. So, while beliefs like *I'm not good enough to do this* are gradually taken to zero, beliefs like *I completely believe in myself and my capabilities* are taken to 100 percent. Both sides of the equation are important. In advanced versions of Enlightened Transformation, beliefs are optimized at six levels: Conscious, Subconscious, Genetic, History, Collective, and Soul.

- Spirit—Level of Connection and Consciousness:

Level of Connection with Spirit, God, Source, Yahweh, Jesus, Buddha, Krishna, Creator of All That Is, Divine—whatever you call your Creator—is critical to unleashing and releasing all that you ARE. I put this in all caps, because when your limiting factors are removed, like the excess marble that surrounded the perfection of Michelangelo's David, your connection with Spirit is optimized, and you are truly magnificent and powerful. You are here for an important purpose and now ready to fulfill that mission.

After you have been initiated to the process through the reading of this book, each time *Enlightened Transformation* is used, your connection with Divine will be raised a few measurable points. To put this in perspective, when Dr. David Hawkins published his book, *Power vs Force* in 2002, he indicated that most people never increase their level of consciousness, or Level of Connection, by more than a few points in their lifetime. That was true when he wrote it, but our opportunities are much greater now.

Synergy is unleashed only when we address all three factors: Body, Mind, and Spirit. Remember, it's like 1 + 1 + 1 = 30.

BREAKTHROUGH

This is really powerful!

I have to say this particular thing [Enlightened Transformation] is really surprising me. When I first started saying it, I would feel things. It felt powerful, but subtle at the same time. And I feel it is really powerful. It really is making big changes. I appreciate all you're doing, but this particular piece is surprising to me how simple and easy it is.

~ Ron S., Life Coach

IMPORTANT NOTE:

Reading this book serves to initiate you, or activate you, to use our Primary process for yourself. *It will not be effective for someone who has not read the book*. Please share this book with family members, friends, or colleagues so they can also begin this process. Let them know that it will work only if they read the book!

Reading this book is a conscious learning experience that activates the *Enlightened Transformation Primary* process for the reader. Knowing how this evolved is important, even if you don't fully understand it. In addition, it will not work for you to use it for anyone other than yourself. We'll discuss that further in the next section.

The Enlightened Transformation Primary Version: A 3-Step Process

Before we get to the 3-Step process, I want to introduce the *Primary Clearing List*. The Primary Clearing List is a list that we keep and continually modify and enhance, and calling it out in the process is all that is required. This Primary Clearing List includes thousands of limiting and empowering beliefs, as well as emotional factors that might be keeping you from being your best. We will add to this list over time. You can also create your own list and simply refer to it. That's an important factor as they are your words, your energy.

The actual *Enlightened Transformation Primary* process continues to evolve. For more information, see the Next Steps section at the end of this book for links to download this free process.

Here is a big picture of the process:

1. Express gratitude for all your blessings.

2. State what you want with this request, including the Primary Clearing List that we continue to update.

3. Express gratitude for this enhancement.

Do you realize how important *gratitude* is?

If you're as conscious as I think you are, you have already realized just how important gratitude is, so it's not surprising that gratitude bookends the request.

How is that for simplicity?

Of course, much of the request comes from the Primary Clearing List.

Download the *Enlightened Transformation Primary* process, use it, and experience the value over the next few days or weeks. If you want to go further, advanced versions and additional help are available through the work of *Life's New Game*. See the link to our website in the Next Steps section of the book.

BIOLOGICAL AGE: CHRONOLOGICAL VERSUS EFFECTIVE

What is your age?

Your chronological age tells you how long it has been since you were born, but there are other ways to view and assess age.

There is much talk about how long we can expect to live. Statisticians are always developing methods for predicting how old each of us will be when we die. You cannot help but be impacted by these expectations. They often become subconscious beliefs, and these beliefs contribute to your body's deterioration as you age.

How I Discovered Effective Biological Age

After my autoimmune system was spontaneously healed, I started noticing, as time went on, that I was continuing to get healthier and healthier. I felt *younger* than I had felt for many years. It occurred to me that chronological age is only one way of measuring age. Another term popped into my head—*Effective Biological Age* (EBA)—that seemed to describe what I was thinking in the moment. Your health would determine your EBA, and it may be very different from your chronological age.

I wondered if I could energetically measure it the same way, kinesiologically, that I had been using to measure everything in my work and life. Well, yes!—I could, or at least my EBA was measuring significantly lower than my calendar age.

So, I started measuring EBA for my clients and found the more clearing we did, the lower EBA gradually became over the time I worked with them. This made sense to me, as the thousands of trapped emotions that were burdening our bodies were being released, but I did not have proof.

One day, I was having lunch with my client of a few months, Kelly.

During the meal, Kelly said, "I had a doctor's appointment today, and she told me my Effective Biological Age!"

"What!?" I exclaimed, totally shocked that she was using terminology that I thought was mine, yet I had not shared. "Don't tell me what she said, please!"

I then used my energy measurement method to carefully measure what I got for her EBA.

I said, "I get your Effective Biological Age as forty-one years old. What did Doctor Eriksen say?"

Kelly said, laughingly, "Obviously, the doctor is right. She got effective age of forty years old!"

Wow! The doctor and I responded with ages only one year apart. More importantly, after a few months of *Life's New Game*, Kelly's EBA was fourteen years younger than her chronological age of fifty-four at the time. And her EBA continued to drop even after our work together because she continued to use the *Enlightened Transformation* process.

Soon, another client, Mary, went to Dr. Eriksen for a checkup and came away with the identical EBA that I had measured, which was twenty-four years younger than her calendar age. She had been doing this work longer. I love it when the science backs up the energy measurement.

The Surprise Wellness Benefits

Some clients were reporting that aches and pains were going away, and physical abilities that tend to deteriorate with age were coming back—literally. So, I started tracking their wellness breakthroughs by testing EBA—though I didn't actually know *what* I was tracking. I just tracked it to correlate the events that occurred with continued use of *Enlightened Transformation*— clearing of emotional baggage, shifting beliefs, and Level of Connection with Divine, and any coincidental changes in

EBA. Note that we are not in the healthcare business in any way, and we do not claim any health benefits will occur.

BREAKTHROUGH

I'm so grateful I decided to work with you.

Ed, when I called you for a private session on November 7, I told you that, while I had a total of five clients from January to the end of August, from September to early November alone, I had eight clients and five more in the pipeline waiting for agreements. It is amazing how they are showing up. Also, the quality is phenomenal; the relationships are great and should bring even more business. It's a lot of work, yet I'm not overwhelmed! I couldn't be more pleased with working with you. Thank you.

I had come to you before with a separate issue, saying "Now if you can just solve this one problem, you'll be my hero forever!"

You asked what it was, and I told you that my right hip and knee were very painful, making it hard to get in and out of the car, and if I sat more than 30 minutes, I had a hard time getting up. I told you the pain level was a 6 or 7 out of 10.

You said, "You know, I'm not a doctor or any kind of healthcare practitioner, so I can only facilitate the release of emotions that might be related to those physical issues and see what happens."

Within thirty minutes, you had cleared the major emotional trauma in both the knee and hip without any help from me—childhood traumas I could relate to—and the pain was down to 2 or 3. You said to monitor it and let you know what happened over the next few days.

My text to you the following day was PAIN LEVEL 1–2. The following day was 0.5 to 1. It's been months now, and I haven't had any pain at all. Your work is amazing. And knowing that my Effective Biological Age is down to fifty-one and continuing to drop is super-encouraging [chronological age seventy-six], and it is showing up physically as more and more of my excessive weight just drops away. I'm so grateful I decided to work with you, and it's also great to call you my friend.

~ Phil B., Executive Coach and Consultant

THE BENEFIT OF *LIFE'S NEW GAME* FOR YOUR CLIENTS

As you realize the power of *Life's New Game* in unleashing all your own talents and capabilities, you might realize the value this could be for people you work and live with.[3*]

Using this Program to Raise the Performance of Others

Gayle was certified to do this work for her coaching clients.[4**] She kept telling us how important and easy it was to add *Life's New Game* to her coaching.

"My clients are the ones getting promoted," she told us.

Then one day, she called to share the story of how the senior vice president—who many of her clients worked for—wanted to speak with her. They spent fifteen minutes or so enjoyably discussing the breakthroughs her direct reports, Gayle's clients, were having. Toward the end of the meeting, the executive leaned toward Gayle and asked, "Would you consider coaching me?"

Would you consider coaching me?!

Do you get the significance of that?

---

3   *Initiation and Certification are required to use this program and advanced processes to help other people. We offer certification training and initiation if that would serve you. See Next Steps for details.

4   **Full disclosure: the version of *Enlightened Transformation* Gayle is certified to use with her clients is a highly advanced version to release their limitations and enhance their strengths. While they are becoming more and more of their true selves, she is providing exceptional coaching for how to best use their talents.

Do you coach, mentor, or consult in your business?

If you become certified and initiated to use the process for others, and invest just a few minutes a day to release the limitations and unleash the talents of those people, what do you think it would do for them?

As their Bodies, Minds, and Spirits are gradually optimized, what would it mean for their lives, their businesses, and their families?

What would it do for your business and your life?

Conclusion

For the last six years, I have been on a journey of learning, inspired insight, breakthrough realizations, and healing. And it continues. The extent of my healing has only been briefly revealed in this writing. The person I am today is so different from who I was just six years ago. I am proud of the person I have become and continue to become.

More importantly, I know that *you* are much more than you currently show up to be. You are alive at this time for an important purpose, a purpose that only you can fulfill. If you are hearing a big wake-up call right now, it is because our fragile planet needs your unique talent; it is the reason that you have been here all along.

Remember this: *The privilege of a lifetime is becoming who you were meant to be.*

May we assist you in your journey?

If it feels right, reach out to us. We would love to connect with you.

When your limitations have been removed, when your connection with the Divine is optimized, when your strengths have been fortified, your role in enhancing lives of others will be revealed, if it has not been revealed already. And, as you become more and more of the special, unique person you are, as you make that important difference, how fulfilling life will be!

I know this to be true from my own experience and from the experiences of scores of clients. I hope to hear about the difference you are making. Blessings for health, wealth, and freedom, as you move forward with your unique contribution.

Next Steps

Well, you now have a brief overview of what I had learned from the time I began this journey up until the time this book was written. It was difficult to stop writing so we could publish because the learning never stops. If you'd like to catch up with the latest breakthrough realizations, check out my website: lifesnewgame.com for additional information. Browse around the site for new articles and videos.

How to Get Enlightened Transformation™

To download the latest Primary version of *Enlightened Transformation*, go to: lifesnewgame.com/ETPrimary. This book provides sufficient assistance for achieving this Primary level of transformation.

Would you like to consider working with us to optimize your own life and contribution?

We would be honored to speak with you about your situation and whether *Life's New Game* would be a good fit for you. This program is intended for busy people who don't have a lot of spare time, so we do most of the work for you. Your time commitment averages only 7 minutes a day for 12 weeks. And that's to become your true, Ideal Self, the person you were born to be, so you can live the blessed life you were intended to live and make the difference you were born to make. Please schedule a discussion about your situation and what we offer at lifesnewgame.com/schedule.

Are you a coach, consultant, or healer?

Might you be interested in adding *Life's New Game* to the value you already provide your clients? It takes only a few minutes a day of your time to accelerate the Body, Mind, and Spirit breakthroughs of your clients utilizing *Enlightened Transformation Advanced*. Contact us to discuss the requirements and value of certification: lifesnewgame.com/schedule.

Appendix

Energy Measurement or Applied Kinesiology

Energy measurement is a powerful skill to develop. Here are some *Life's New Game* approved videos to help.

Truth Testing: How to Use a Pendulum: Part I.
youtu.be/dTPk9iEw0-s.

Perelandra Kinesiology Testing Technique.
youtu.be/dTPk9iEw0-s.

Theta Healing Muscle Sway Test.
youtu.be/6wxBLW38ZBU.

AK or Applied Kinesiology: Part I.
youtu.be/aUfWJKi0E60.

References

Carlson, Edwin C. *Creating a SOLID Self: Core Health Series 1 & 2.* Core Health Publishing, 2010.

Carlson, Edwin C. *Heart Forgiveness: Creating Freedom.* Core Health Publishing, 2009.

Diamond, John. *Your Body Doesn't Lie: Unlock the Power of Your Natural Energy.* Warner Books, 1979.

Hawkins, David R. *Power vs Force: The Hidden Determinants of Human Behavior.* Hay House, 2012.

Lloyd, Alexander. *The Healing Code: 6 Minutes to Heal the Source of Your Health, Success, or Relationship Issue.* Hachette Book Group, 2010.

Nelson, Bradley B. *The Emotion Code: How to Release Your Trapped Emotions for Abundant Health, Love and Happiness.* Wellness Unmasked Publishing, 2007.

Oakley, Ed, and Doug Krug. *Enlightened Leadership: Getting to the Heart of Change.* Simon & Schuster, 1994.

Oakley, Ed. *Be a Trusted Leader: Accelerate Your Influence Now!* Enlightened Leadership Publications, 2012.

Slatter, Jean. *Hiring the Heavens: A Practical Guide to Developing Working Relationships with the Spirits of Creation.* Jean Slatter, 2003.

St. John, Noah. *Afformations: The Miracle of Positive Self-Talk.* Hay House, 2013.

Stibal, Vianna. *Theta Healing: Introducing an Extraordinary Energy Healing Modality.* Rolling Thunder Publishing, 2010.

West, Linda. *Secrets the Secret Never Told You: How to Use the Law of Attraction.* Linda West, 2010.

Williams, Robert M. *PSYCH-K . . . The Missing ~~Piece~~ Peace in Your Life.* The Myrddin Corporation, 2009.

About the Author

Armed with an electrical engineering degree from North Carolina State University and a master's degree from Stanford, Ed quickly rose into the executive ranks of Hewlett-Packard. The ability that best served him then—and today—is his natural talent to see and merge multiple perspectives and ideas into simple, effective solutions to complex challenges.

That talent proved critical when Ed started his own leadership development company over thirty years ago. Using his talent to learn from many resources and create a simplified, more effective framework, Ed co-authored the best-selling Simon & Schuster book, *Enlightened Leadership: Getting to the Heart of Change*, which has sold over 295,000 copies. That book was arguably the first book promoting true collaboration—so important for moving forward in today's world.

Ed and his teams worked with twenty-three of the Fortune 100 companies, developing leaders from sixty-seven countries before his own life took a mid-life detour that he wasn't sure he was going to survive. Unexpectedly, he had a profound experience that led to a spontaneous healing.

What he learned in the process has not only taken his life to new levels of ability and well-being, but has benefitted many clients faced with mid-life detours as well. Many have experienced personal and business breakthroughs that are allowing them to make a much bigger difference while enjoying their lives, family, and more freedom than ever.

Ed's intention at this stage of his life is simple—to see how many conscious people he can mentor to breakthroughs in every aspect of their lives, including making a bigger difference in the world.

www.ingramcontent.com/pod-product-compliance
Lightning Source LLC
Chambersburg PA
CBHW062009040426
42447CB00010B/1979